USING THIS BOOK

*One of the best ways of helping children to learn to read is by reading stories to them and with them. This way they learn what **reading** is, and they will gradually come to recognise many words, and begin to read for themselves.*

First, grown-ups read the story on the left-hand pages aloud to the child.

You can reread the story as often as the child enjoys hearing it. Talk about the pictures as you go.

Later the child will read the words under the pictures on the right-hand page.

The pages at the back of the book will give you some ideas for helping your child to read.

British Library Cataloguing in Publication Data
McCullagh, Sheila K.
    The flying saucer. — (Puddle Lane. Series no. 855.
    Stage 1; v. 7)
    I. Title   II. Morris, Tony   III. Series
    823'.914[J]   PZ7
    ISBN 0-7214-0912-1

First edition

Published by Ladybird Books Ltd Loughborough Leicestershire UK
Ladybird Books Inc Lewiston Maine 04240 USA
© Text and layout SHEILA McCULLAGH MCMLXXXV
© In publication LADYBIRD BOOKS LTD MCMLXXXV

The flying saucer

written by SHEILA McCULLAGH
illustrated by TONY MORRIS

This book belongs to:

Ladybird Books

Tessa Catchamouse was a little grey cat.
She had white paws, and white whiskers.
She lived in a hole
in a very old house.

She lived there with her mother,
whose name was Pegs,
and her brother,
whose name was Tim.

Tessa

A magician lived in the top room
of the house.

The rest of the house was empty.

the Magician

One day, Tessa climbed up a tree.
She jumped on to the roof
of the house.

There was a window in the roof.
The window was open.

Tessa looked in through the window.
The room was empty.
There was no one there.

Tessa looked in.

There was a long pole
leaning against the window.
Tessa climbed down the pole.

She ran across to the Magician's chair.
It was near a big table.

Tessa jumped up on to the chair.

Tessa jumped up
on to the chair.

She jumped from the chair
to the table.

Tessa jumped on to
the table.

There was a big saucer
standing on the table.

The saucer had strange red and
green patterns on it.

There were two words on the saucer.
But Tessa couldn't read yet,
so she didn't know
what the words were.

the saucer

Tessa stepped into the saucer,
to have a better look at it.

She didn't notice a little red button
in the bottom of the saucer.
She put her paw
right on the button.

Tessa in the saucer

The moment Tessa touched the button,
the saucer flew up into the air!

The saucer flew up.

Tessa was excited.
"It's a flying saucer!"
she cried.
"I wish it would fly somewhere!"
And at once, the saucer flew
out of the window.

It flew over the roof,
and over the garden.

The saucer flew out
of the window.

The saucer flew over the streets.

It flew over the houses
in the town.

The saucer flew on and on.

The saucer flew
on and on.

At first, Tessa was very excited.

She went to the rim of the saucer,
and looked at the houses below.

"I'd like to stop for a bit," she said.
"I'd like to look at the houses."

But the saucer flew on and on.

The saucer flew
on and on.

Tessa began to feel frightened.

"Miaow!" she cried.
"I want to go home!
I want to go back to the house!"

But the saucer flew on and on.

The saucer flew
on and on.

The saucer flew over the park.
It flew on, over the river.

"Miaow!" cried Tessa.
"I want to go home!"

But the saucer flew on and on.

The saucer flew
on and on.

"Oh dear," cried Tessa.
"I **wish** I was home!"
And she sat down
on the little red button.

Tessa sat down.

The saucer spun round
and round and round,
and Tessa almost fell off.
Then the saucer stopped spinning,
and started off again.

Tessa almost fell off.

The saucer flew back over the park.

It flew back over the river.
It flew back to the old house
where Tessa lived.

The saucer flew back
to the old house.

The saucer flew down to earth
very slowly.

It landed just outside the hole
in the steps, where Tessa lived.
Tessa jumped out of the saucer,
and the flying saucer flew up again,
back to the attic
where the Magician lived.

The saucer flew down.

Pegs was just coming in
under the garden gate,
as Tessa flew down in the saucer.

"Tessa!" cried Pegs.
"Where **have** you been?"

"I've been for a ride," said Tessa.
"But I'm so glad to be home!"

"I should think you are!"
said Pegs.

Pegs saw Tessa.

Notes for the parent/teacher

When you have read the story, go back to the beginning. Look at each picture and talk about it, pointing to the caption below, and reading it aloud yourself.

Run your finger along under the words as you read, so that the child learns that reading goes from left to right. (You needn't say this in so many words. Children learn many useful things about reading by just reading with you, and it is often better to let them learn by experience, rather than by explanation.) When you next go through the book, encourage the child to read the words and sentences under the illustrations.

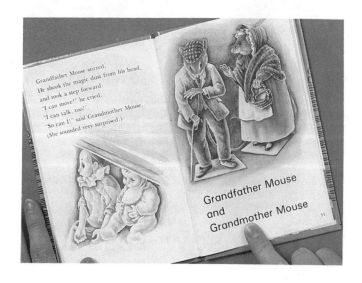

Grandfather Mouse stirred.
He shook the magic dust from his head,
and took a step forward.
"I can move!" he cried.
"I can talk, too!"
"So can I!" said Grandmother Mouse.
(She sounded very surprised.)

Grandfather Mouse and Grandmother Mouse

Don't rush in with the word before he* has time to think, but don't leave him struggling for too long. Always encourage him to feel that he is reading successfully, praising him when he does well, and avoiding criticism.

Now turn back to the beginning, and print the child's name in the space on the title page, using ordinary, not capital letters. Let him watch you print it: this is another useful experience.

*Children enjoy hearing the same story many times. Read this one as often as the child likes hearing it. The more opportunities he has of looking at the illustrations and **reading** the captions with you, the more he will come to recognise the words. Don't worry if he **remembers** rather than **reads** the captions. This is a normal stage in learning.*

If you have a number of books, let him choose which story he would like to have again.

**Footnote:* In order to avoid the continual "he or she", "him or her", the child is referred to in this book as "he". However, the stories are equally appropriate for girls and boys.

*Ask the child first to look at the pictures
and read the words, and then to cover the
pictures and read the words again.*

Tessa

the
Magician

the saucer

the Magician's house

Puddle Lane Reading Programme   **Stage 1**

There are several books at this Stage about the same characters. All the books at each Stage are separate stories and are written at the same reading level.

There are more stories about Tessa and Tim and the Magician in these books:

from
When the magic stopped